To ....

From ....

Other books by Gregory E. Lang:

WHY A DAUGHTER NEEDS A DAD

WHY A SON NEEDS A MOM

WHY A SON NEEDS A DAD

WHY I LOVE GRANDMA

WHY I LOVE GRANDPA

WHY I CHOSE YOU

WHY I LOVE YOU

WHY MY HEART STILL SKIPS A BEAT

WHY A BABY NEEDS A MOMMY

WHY WE ARE A FAMILY

WHY WE ARE FRIENDS

GOOD LUCK, GRADUATE

BROTHERS AND SISTERS

SIMPLE ACTS

LOVE SIGNS

LIFE MAPS

THANK YOU, MOM

THANK YOU, DAD

BECAUSE YOU ARE MY DAUGHTER

BECAUSE YOU ARE MY SON

WHY A

Son

NEEDS A

Mom

100 REASONS

Gregory E. Lang

CUMBERLAND HOUSE

Published by Cumberland House, an imprint of Sourcebooks, Inc.
P.O. Box 4410, Naperville, Illinois 60567–4410
(630) 961–3900 Fax: (630) 961–2168
www.sourcebooks.com

Printed and bound in China
OGP 10 9 8 7 6 5 4 3 2 1

On behalf of my brothers,
David, Kevin, and Jody, and myself,
this book is lovingly dedicated to
Gloria Dianne Brown Lang,
our mom.

· INTRODUCTION ·

On my mantelpiece rests an aging photograph of my mother that was taken as she was about to graduate from high school, a few short years before she chose to alter her life and become a mother. She was beautiful then, with hair that fell upon her shoulders, big eyes that reassured, and a smile that warmed. I am told she was energetic, vivacious, and popular back then, when she was young and had only herself to be concerned about. This photograph is my favorite picture of my mother, and although it has yellowed and faded, it has been lovingly displayed wherever I have lived and serves to remind me of the nest from which I flew, the home my mother kept for my four siblings and me, and the bosom to which I always return—one of unconditional love and acceptance.

My memories of childhood include the many things my mother did to make sure my siblings and I were well cared for and happy. Every day began with a hot breakfast, often including biscuits made from scratch, lunch boxes were filled with what we each liked to eat, and dinner always included someone's favorite food. With a family so large, cooking consumed much of her time. My passion for cooking and belief that it is a sincere gesture of love can be traced back to my mother and the way she never failed to bake a birthday cake of choice, bring soup to the child sick in bed, alter recipes to suit our tastes, and make the house smell like the approaching season or holiday. But my mother did far more than cook for us to let us know she loved us.

She made clothes for us, tended to our scrapes and cuts, drove us to our respective after-school activities and cheered us on, sought out obscure but coveted gifts for Christmas, helped with difficult homework assignments, wiped tears away and endured tantrums, all the while making sure not a child was overlooked, doing or giving whatever each needed, as though she had nothing more important to do. My mother helped me negotiate my conflicts with my dad, taught me to ride a bicycle, balance a checkbook, sew on a button, check a turkey for doneness, change a diaper, treat a cold, and, years later, how to determine what my own infant needed when she cried. My mother did many other things for me that taken one at a time may seem inconsequential, but when taken all together, made me who I am. She also did things for me that others are unaware of, and knowing her, I am confident I am not alone in that privilege. But still, my mother did far more than these kinds of everyday maternal tasks to let us know she loved us.

Each son eventually presented our parents with a unique set of challenges, and my mother was unfailing in her ability to deal with what came. If she was ever disappointed in us, any sign of it was overshadowed by her actions. One son got into trouble, and my mother was there to help him find a different path. One fell on hard times, and my mother was there to help ease the burden until times got better. Another could not see beyond a broken heart, and my mother was there to offer comfort and bring hope. One child became sick, and my mother was there to provide care. Our mother has loved us collectively, but also individually in a way that expresses to each of us, in the way that only a mother can express, that she is, and shall remain, there for us, no matter what. Gone from her nest but never from her heart, fully grown but always her beloved son or little girl, each can call upon her still, and she will come. It is this, her unwavering devotion, her tireless effort to help, her unshakable faith in our goodness, her absolute belief in our worth, that let us know then and lets us know now, that we are loved.

I am the first of five children, and over the forty-plus years since my birth I have seen much about my mother change, and I have seen much remain the same. Although now much older than the young woman pictured in the photograph I treasure, her eyes still offer reassurance to whomever she gazes upon, as does the gentle touch she gives while listening intently to whatever one shares with her. Her smile still warms, as does her laughter and the heartfelt embrace all have come to expect when coming upon her. I still receive birthday cards, enjoy a favorite meal when I go home, and hear from her the applause and affirmations that tell me she is proud of my accomplishments. Now walking more slowly, her hands less able than they once were, her health requiring more and more concessions from her, she struggles at times to keep up her former pace. Yet, in spite of these changes, she always manages to be there when needed.

I do not know what my mother's dreams were, what plans she had in mind for herself as she grew up, where she wanted to visit or what she might have become if she had chosen to live her life differently. I am ashamed that I do not know these things because I have never thought to ask, but I also do not know because my mother has never uttered a word of disappointment about the life she has lived. I do not know of her regrets for she does not share them, if they exist, nor does she lament about what her life used to be like or otherwise give off signs of disappointment about what age has taken from her. Perhaps she has just accepted her life for what it is, thinking it is too late to change it. Or, perhaps she is happy with her life for what it has been. It is the latter, I like to think, because I know my mother has enjoyed being a mother, and a grandmother, and a surrogate mother or grandmother to those in need who have been fortunate enough to enter her life. I know this because she never fails to seize the opportunity to act like a mom, to be there for someone.

I love my mother dearly, and I have a long list of things I want to do for her one day, but most of all I want to tell her "thank you." I believe that a child, especially a son, can never express enough gratitude for what a mother has done. I know that I cannot, but I know what I will do to try. I will do what my mother did for me. I will be there when she needs me, no matter what. I love you, Mom.

WHY A

Son

NEEDS A

Mom

A

Son

· *Needs a* ·

MOM

....

to tell him he is handsome.

....

A

Son

· *Needs a* ·

MOM

TO HELP HIM UNDERSTAND THAT THINGS
WILL NOT ALWAYS GO HIS WAY.

·

*to teach him that not every fight
is worth fighting.*

·

TO ASSURE HIM THAT HIS HEARTACHE
WILL NOT LAST FOREVER.

A

Son

· Needs a ·

MOM

to teach him that embarrassment
is not a reason for quitting.

··

TO TEACH HIM TO PLAY FAIR.

··

to help him see the
richness of diversity.

A

Son

· *Needs a* ·

MOM

WHO SEES THE HUMOR
IN HIS SILLY WAYS.

·

who insists that he do his fair
share of the household chores.

·

WHO WILL STAND UP TO HIM
WHEN HE IS WRONG.

A

Son

· *Needs a* ·

MOM

....

to see that he does not become spoiled.

....

A

Son

· *Needs a* ·

MOM

TO BELIEVE IN HIM EVEN WHEN IT
SEEMS NO ONE ELSE DOES.

·

*to teach him to pay attention
to the small things.*

·

TO TEACH HIM TO SHOW APPRECIATION
FOR WHAT OTHERS HAVE DONE FOR HIM.

A

Son

· Needs a ·

MOM

*to make sure he looks his
best before leaving the house.*

TO MAKE SURE THAT FAITH IS
THE LIGHT THAT GUIDES HIM.

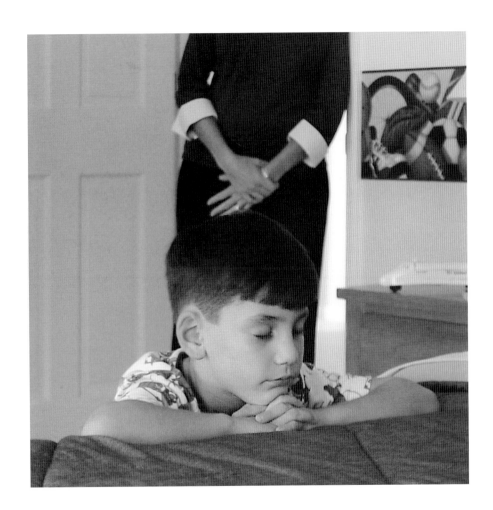

A

Son

· *Needs a* ·

MOM

TO TELL HIM THAT ANYTHING IS POSSIBLE
IF DONE FOR THE RIGHT REASON.

·

*to tell him that remaining faithful
is his promise and obligation.*

·

TO BE HIS TRUSTED CONFIDANTE.

A

Son

· *Needs a* ·

MOM

....

who encourages self-expression.

....

A

Son

· Needs a ·

MOM

TO MAKE SURE HE ATTENDS TO HIS MIND,
AS WELL AS HIS BODY.

*to teach him that all people
are worthy of respect.*

A

Son

· *Needs a* ·

MOM

to help him overcome his fears.

··

WHO WILL NOT FAIL TO DISCIPLINE
HIM FOR HIS MISDEEDS.

··

A

Son

· *Needs a* ·

MOM

TO HELP HIM UNDERSTAND
AND RESPECT PERSONAL SPACE.

·

to help him learn how to laugh at himself.

·

TO HELP HIM DEVELOP
THE HABITS OTHERS PRIZE.

A

Son

Needs a

MOM

WHO IS NEVER MORE THAN

A PHONE CALL AWAY.

·

to remind him to say his prayers.

A

Son

· *Needs a* ·

MOM

*to teach him that he can be
competitive without being ruthless.*

·····································

TO TEACH HIM TO AVOID
SELFISH TEMPTATIONS.

·····································

A

Son

· *Needs a* ·

MOM

TO TEACH HIM TO TRY HARDER
WHEN GIVEN A SECOND CHANCE.

*to teach him that family is
more important than work.*

A

Son

· *Needs a* ·

MOM

to make sure his world
has a broad horizon.

A

Son

· *Needs a* ·

MOM

WHO UNDERSTANDS THE PLEASURE
OF A GOOD PILLOW FIGHT.

....

to be his first dance partner.

....

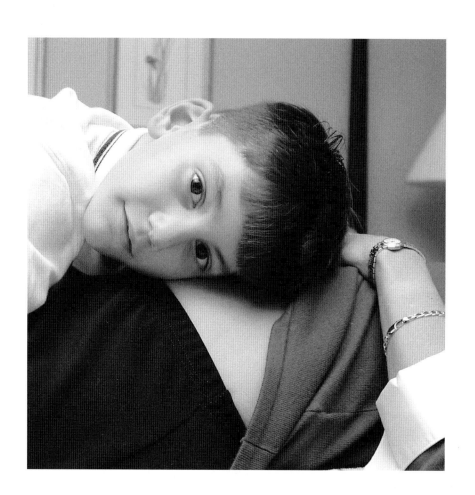

A

Son

· Needs a ·

MOM

*to help him understand
the secrets of girls.*

···

TO TELL HIM ABOUT

THE MIRACLE OF LIFE.

···

A

Son

Needs a

MOM

WHO WILL INDULGE HIS LOVE OF ACTION.

*who allows him to be
her protector now and then.*

A

Son

· *Needs a* ·

MOM

to steer him away from darkness.

....

TO BE HIS STRENGTH WHEN HE IS WEAK.

....

A

Son

· *Needs a* ·

MOM

TO TEACH HIM THAT ADMITTING
ONE'S MISTAKES IS A SIGN
OF STRENGTH, NOT WEAKNESS.

·

*to tell him that he cannot change
others, but he can learn to accept
them for who they are.*

A

Son

· Needs a ·

MOM

....

to protect him until he is old
enough to protect himself.

....

A

Son

· Needs a ·

MOM

·······························

TO MAKE SURE HIS SOCKS MATCH.

·······························

*who knows where to find what
he has misplaced.*

A

Son

· *Needs a* ·

MOM

TO TEACH HIM HOW TO FLIRT WITHOUT
MAKING A FOOL OF HIMSELF.

·

*to teach him that being subtle
can be attractive.*

A

Son

· *Needs a* ·

MOM

who will let him be himself.

....

TO MAKE SURE HE HAS GOOD
MEMORIES TO HOLD ON TO.

....

A

Son

Needs a

MOM

TO MAKE HIS FAVORITE FOOD
ON HIS BIRTHDAY.

*who leads him toward his
talents and passions.*

A

Son

· Needs a ·

MOM

· ·

to make sure he begins his
day on the right foot.

· ·

A

Son

· Needs a ·

MOM

....

to teach him to take care of himself.

....

A

Son

· Needs a ·

MOM

TO SHOW HIM HOW TO TAKE

ONE DAY AT A TIME.

·

to teach him that sometimes
the battle is within.

A

Son

· Needs a ·

MOM

who laughs at his jokes.

A

Son

· Needs a ·

MOM

who does not hold him back when
he is ready to take the next step.

·

WHO IS THERE FOR HIM NO
MATTER WHAT HIS AGE.

A

Son

· Needs a ·

MOM

···

who will make sure he does
not get lost in the crowd.

···

A

Son

· *Needs a* ·

MOM

TO LET HIM KNOW
IT IS OKAY TO CRY.

·

*to show him what it means
to love unconditionally.*

·

TO TELL HIM OFTEN
THAT HE IS LOVED.

A

Son

· *Needs a* ·

MOM

··

who understands that
boys like big toys.

··

A

Son

· Needs a ·

MOM

who will let him go when
he is ready to marry.

·

TO HELP PREPARE HIM FOR

BEING A FATHER.

A

Son

· Needs a ·

MOM

....

to teach him the art of listening.

....

A

Son

· *Needs a* ·

MOM

TO INSIST THAT HE BE
RESPECTFUL OF WOMEN.

·

*to teach him to be a force
of kindness in the world.*

·

TO TEACH HIM THE
PITFALLS OF HYPOCRISY.

A

Son

· Needs a ·

MOM

....

who is always excited
to hear his news.

....

A

Son

· *Needs a* ·

MOM

TO TEACH HIM THAT

HE SHOULD BE HUMBLE.

·

to teach him table manners.

·

TO HELP HIM DEVELOP

SOUND FINANCIAL HABITS.

A

Son

· *Needs a* ·

MOM

....

to make sure there is no room
for bitterness in his heart.

....

A

Son

· Needs a ·

MOM

WHO IS ALWAYS THERE

FOR HIM, EVEN IF BY EMAIL.

·

who will always make sure
he has a home to come back to.

·

TO TELL HIM THAT EVERYONE

ADMIRES A SINCERE APOLOGY.

A

Son

· Needs a ·

MOM

to fill his childhood with
love and affection.

A

Son

· Needs a ·

MOM

TO ADVISE HIM WHEN

HE FALLS IN LOVE.

·

to explain to him what he
cannot yet understand.

·

TO TELL HIM THAT THERE IS MORE

TO BEING A MAN THAN BEING TOUGH.

A

Son

· Needs a ·

MOM

to teach him that a sense of
humor will never lose its luster.

A

Son

· Needs a ·

MOM

WHOSE ARMS, HEART, AND MIND
ARE ALWAYS OPEN.

·

who doesn't forget that
boys will be boys.

·

WHO KNOWS HOW TO HAVE FUN.

A

Son

· *Needs a* ·

MOM

to tell him that jealousy
can ruin a relationship.

A

Son

· *Needs a* ·

MOM

TO ENCOURAGE HIM TO BE
SERIOUS ABOUT HIS WORK.

·

*to make sacrifices so he will
not have to sacrifice.*

·

TO TEACH HIM THE IMPORTANCE
OF COMPROMISE.

A

Son

· Needs a ·

MOM

....

to hold him when he needs comfort.

....

A

Son

· *Needs a* ·

MOM

....

to make sure he finishes
his homework.

....

A

Son

· *Needs a* ·

MOM

TO TEACH HIM HOW TO CONDUCT
HIMSELF LIKE A GENTLEMAN.

*to teach him how to show
love without restraint.*

A

Son

· *Needs a* ·

MOM

∙∙

who understands that what he needs
from her changes as he grows older.

∙∙

A

Son

· Needs a ·

MOM

WHO SHOWS HIM THAT

MEN AND WOMEN ARE EQUALS.

·

who never tires of his hugs and kisses.

·

TO HELP HIM ATTEND TO THE

DETAILS OTHERS WILL NOTICE.

A

Son

· Needs a ·

MOM

································

because without her he will have
less in his life than he deserves.

································

· ACKNOWLEDGMENTS ·

This book could not have been written without the support and generosity of many people. I offer a special thanks to the sons and moms who posed for me, who invited me into their lives and homes, who cooperated with my schedule and sometimes strange requests, and who helped me to better put into words and pictures why sons need their moms.

I also wish to thank the administration of Greater Atlanta Christian School, which helped me once more recruit families to participate in creating this book, Becky Lang who also helped recruit families, and Diane Hileman of Mothers & More, who, although we have never met, extended a great helping hand in finding sons and moms.

Finally, I wish to thank Ron Pitkin and the staff at Cumberland House, including my editor, Lisa Taylor, who once again pushed me to make sure this book became what it could be. I also want to give a special thanks to Julie Jayne, whose faith in each book has been a key contributor to the success of the series. Julie, you have my deepest appreciation and warmest regards.

· TO CONTACT THE AUTHOR ·

Write in care of the publisher:
Gregory E. Lang c/o Sourcebooks, Inc.
P.O. Box 4410
Naperville, IL 60567-4410

Email the author or visit his website:
gregoryelang@gmail.com
www.gregoryelang.com